## Hello, Family Members,

Learning to read is one of the most important accomplishments of early childhood. **Hello Reader!** books are designed to help children become skilled readers who like to read. Beginning readers learn to read by remembering frequently used words like "the," "is," and "and"; by using phonics skills to decode new words; and by interpreting picture and text clues. These books provide both the stories children enjoy and the structure they need to read fluently and independently. Here are suggestions for helping your child *before*, *during*, and *after* reading:

### Before

- Look at the cover and pictures and have your child predict what the story is about.
- Read the story to your child.
- Encourage your child to chime in with familiar words and phrases.
- Echo read with your child by reading a line first and having your child read it after you do.

### During

- Have your child think about a word he or she does not recognize right away. Provide hints such as "Let's see if we know the sounds" and "Have we read other words like this one?"
- Encourage your child to use phonics skills to sound out new words.
- Provide the word for your child when more assistance is needed so that he or she does not struggle and the experience of reading with you is a positive one.
- Encourage your child to have fun by reading with a lot of expression . . . like an actor!

### After

- Have your child keep lists of interesting and favorite words.
- Encourage your child to read the books over and over again. Have him or her read to brothers, sisters, grandparents, and even teddy bears. Repeated readings develop confidence in young readers.
- Talk about the stories. Ask and answer questions. Share ideas about the funniest and most interesting characters and events in the stories.

I do hope that you and your child enjoy this book.

—Francie Alexander
Chief Education Officer,
Scholastic Education

*For Chris and Mim Galligan,*
*tree huggers and leaf lovers*
*—J. Marzollo*

*To the wheels under my cart:*
*Edie, Grace, and Gina*
*—J. Moffatt*

The author and editors would like to thank Fred Gerber,
Queens Botanical Garden, for his expertise.

Cut-paper photography by Paul Dyer.

**Go to www.scholastic.com for Web site information
on Scholastic authors and illustrators.**

Library of Congress Cataloging-in-Publication Data

Marzollo, Jean.
    I am a leaf / by Jean Marzollo; illustrated by Judith Moffatt.
      p.    cm. — (Hello reader! Science. Level 1)
    Summary: A simple introduction to the life cycle and functions of a leaf.
    ISBN 0-590-64120-4
    1. Leaves — Juvenile literature.   [1. Leaves.]   I. Moffatt, Judith, ill.
II. Title.   III. Series.
QK649.M33    1998
581.4'8 — dc21                                         98-5864
                                                          CIP
                                                          AC

10 9 8 7 6 5 4 3 2 1                       02 03 04 05 06

Printed in Singapore     46
This edition first printing, October 2002

# I Am a Leaf

by Jean Marzollo
Illustrated by Judith Moffatt

**Hello Reader! Science — Level 1**

## SCHOLASTIC INC.

New York   Toronto   London   Auckland   Sydney
Mexico City   New Delhi   Hong Kong   Buenos Aires

Hi!
I'm a leaf.
I live on a maple tree.
See the ladybug?
She's crawling on me.
It tickles!

Many leaves live in my tree.
We have a summer job.
We make tree food.

We make it from air
and sunlight.
*Mm-m-m.*
That sun feels good.

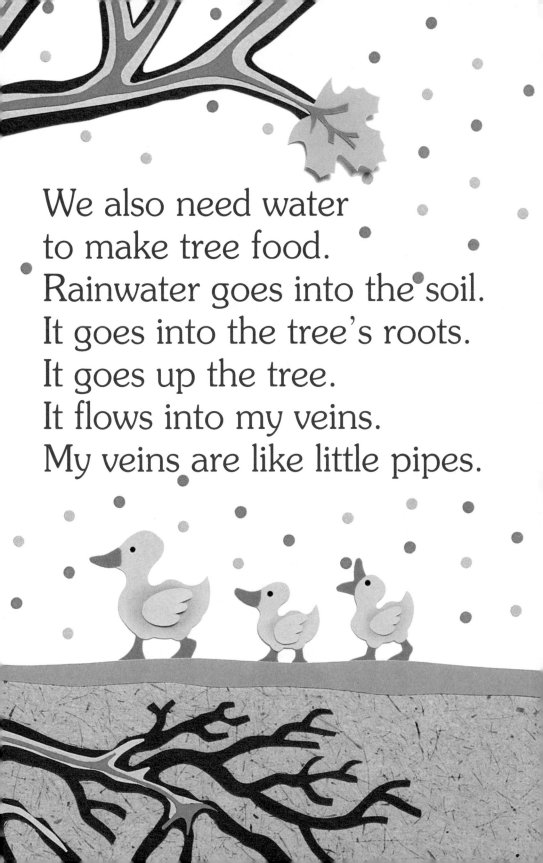

We also need water
to make tree food.
Rainwater goes into the soil.
It goes into the tree's roots.
It goes up the tree.
It flows into my veins.
My veins are like little pipes.

I mix sunlight, air, and water.
Then I add something green.
It's called chlorophyll
(KLOR-o-fill).

Chlorophyll is green.
It makes me green.

All summer long,
I have made tree food.
Once a caterpillar came by.
Nibble.
Nibble.
Nibble.
It ate a little hole in me.
But I still did my job.

Once a spider came by.
Busy.
Busy.
Busy.
It made a big web.
But I still did my job.

Once a squirrel jumped on me.
*Boing!*
*Boing!*
*Boing!*
It ran right over me!
But I still did my job.

Now fall has come.
My work is over.
My green goes away.
Now I am . . .

Red! Yellow! Orange!
It's party time!
All the leaves in my tree
are turning colors!
People *ooh* and *aah*.

The wind blows.
We break away.
We dance with the wind.
*Whee-ee!*
Gently, we land on the ground.

We rest.
Winter has come.
The forest is white with snow.
Some trees stay green.
They are called evergreens.

Slowly, leaves turn into soil.
The soil holds roots.
The soil holds water.
The soil holds animals
sleeping in dens.
Winter is over.
The soil warms.

Hi!
I'm a baby leaf.
Spring is here.
I'm the first bud to sprout
in my tree.

I'm growing fast.
Soon I'll get a job.
What will it be?
*Mm-m-m.*
That sun feels good.

# **MORE ABOUT LEAVES**

Leaves come in many
sizes and shapes.
Most leaves make food
for their plants.
Which leaves are good
for people to eat?
(Salad leaves and spinach
leaves.)

# I Am a Rock

*For Claudio, my rock*
*—J. Marzollo*

*To my* rockin' *friends:*
*Katy, Chris, and Zach*
*—J. Moffatt*

The editors would like to thank Margaret Carruthers
of the American Museum of Natural History,
New York, for her expertise.

Cut-paper photography by Paul Dyer.

Photographs of rock samples on pages 30-31 as follows: Chalk and flint
samples, Breck P. Kent, photographer. Iron sample courtesy of B. Walsh,
J. Beckett, and M. Carruthers. All other rock samples supplied by Photo
Researchers — photographers: granite, Andrew J. Martinez; salt, François
Gohier; gold, Dan Suzio; sandstone, Joyce Photograghics; slate, Aaron Haupt;
diamond, Charles D. Winters; talc, Ben Johnson/Science Photo Library; coal,
Geoff Lane/CSIRO/Science Photo Library; petrified wood, Jim Steinberg.

Library of Congress Cataloging-in-Publication Data
Marzollo, Jean.
        I am a rock / by Jean Marzollo; illustrated by Judith Moffatt.
            p.    cm. — (Hello reader! Level 1)
        Summary: First - person riddles present information about various rocks
and minerals, including sandstone, chalk, slate, and petrified wood.
        ISBN 0-590-37222-X
        1. Rocks — Juvenile literature.    2. Minerals—Juvenile literature.
[1. Rocks — Miscellanea.    2. Minerals—Miscellanea.    3. Questions and
answers.]    I. Moffatt, Judith, ill.    II. Title.    III. Series.
QE432.2.M287  1998
552 — dc21                                                      97-16373
                                                                  CIP
                                                                  AC

# I Am a Rock

by Jean Marzollo
Illustrated by Judith Moffatt

**Hello Reader ! Science — Level 1**

**Cartwheel**
·B·O·O·K·S·®

## SCHOLASTIC INC.

New York   Toronto   London   Auckland   Sydney
Mexico City   New Delhi   Hong Kong   Buenos Aires

Welcome to the
Rock Hall of Fame.
My name is Marble.
Come and meet
my friends.
Can you tell
who they are?

I am a famous granite rock. The Pilgrims stepped on me when they came to America. Who am I?

*Plymouth Rock*

I am white and tasty.
You can sprinkle me
on your food.
Who am I?

*Salt*

# I am used for money and jewelry.
# Who am I?

*Gold*

I am melted
to make glass.
Glassblowers make
shapes from me.
Who am I?

*Sandstone*

You can write with me.
You can draw with me.
Who am I?

*Chalk*

I am flat enough to walk on.
I am flat enough to write on.
Who am I?

*Slate*

I dazzle! I sparkle!
I am a jewel!
I am also very hard.
People use me to cut glass.
Who am I?

*Diamond*

I am ground into powder.
People can shake me on
babies to keep them dry.
Who am I?

*Talc*

I hold heat well.
People use me to
make frying pans and
wood-burning stoves.
If I get wet, I rust.
Who am I?

*Iron*

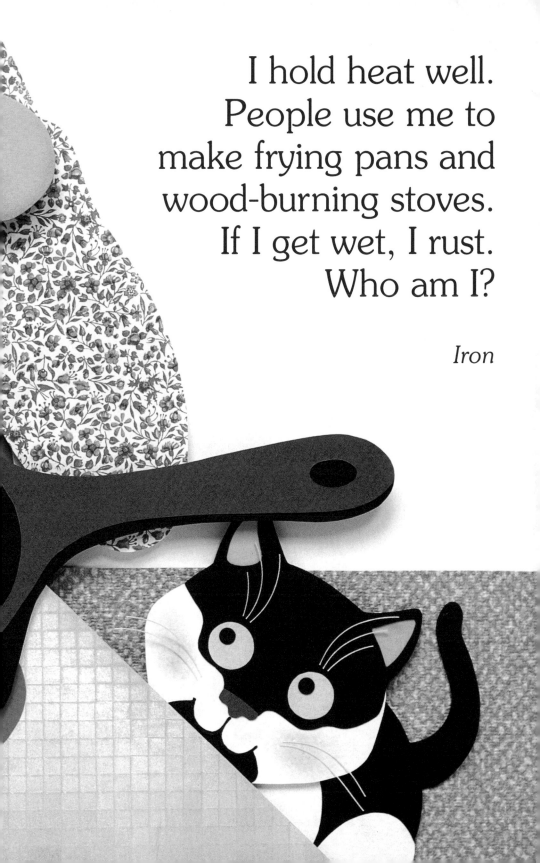

Strike me against a rock.
See the spark?
Campers can use me
to start fires.
Who am I?

*Flint*

I burn slowly.
People can use me
for heat and power.
Who am I?

*Coal*

I look like wood.
I used to *be* wood.
But I am not wood anymore.
Who am I?

*Petrified wood*

# Rocks: Facts and Photos

Rocks are on the ground.
Rocks are under the ground.

Granite

Salt

Gold

Sandstone

Chalk

Slate

Rocks are made of minerals.
Rocks are everywhere on earth.

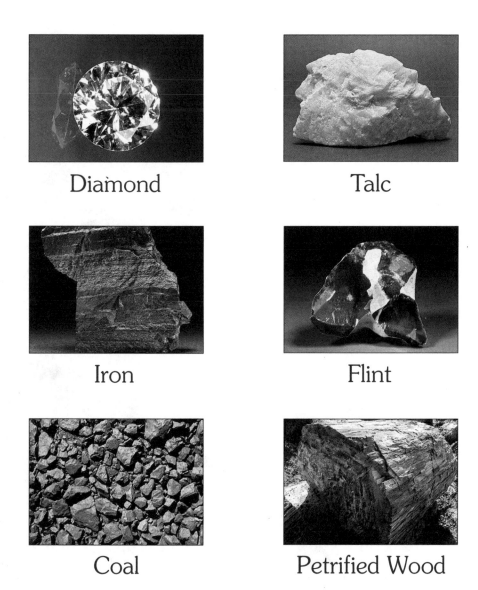

Diamond

Talc

Iron

Flint

Coal

Petrified Wood

Thank you for coming
to the Rock Hall of Fame!
Good-bye.

I Am a Star

*For Erin Claire, who shines like a star.*
*— J. Marzollo*

*For Ruth and Bill, who add sparkle to my life.*
*— J. Moffatt*

Go to www.scholastic.com for Web site information
on Scholastic authors and illustrators.

ISBN 0-439-11320-2

Text copyright © 2000 by Jean Marzollo.
Illustrations copyright © 2000 by Judith Moffatt.
All rights reserved. Published by Scholastic Inc.
SCHOLASTIC, HELLO READER, CARTWHEEL BOOKS, and associated logos
are trademarks and/or registered trademarks of Scholastic Inc.

Library of Congress Cataloging-in-Publication Data

Marzollo, Jean
        I am a star / by Jean Marzollo; illustrated by Judith Moffatt.
                p. cm. — (Hello reader! science — Level 1)
        Summary: Introduces stars and how they appear in the night sky.
        ISBN 0-439-11320-2 (pbk.)
        1. Stars — Juvenile literature. [1. Stars.] I. Moffatt, Judith, ill. II. Title. III. Series
QB801.7.M386 2000
523.8 — dc21                                                    99-046436

# I Am a Star

by Jean Marzollo
Illustrated by Judith Moffatt

## Hello Reader! Science—Level 1

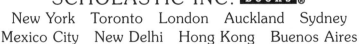

SCHOLASTIC INC. Cartwheel BOOKS®
New York   Toronto   London   Auckland   Sydney
Mexico City   New Delhi   Hong Kong   Buenos Aires

I am a star.

You can't see me
in the daytime.
There is too much light.

You can't see me
on a cloudy night.
I hide behind clouds.

You can see stars
on a clear night.
Long ago, people
saw pictures in stars.

The pictures are
called constellations
[con-stel-A-shuns].

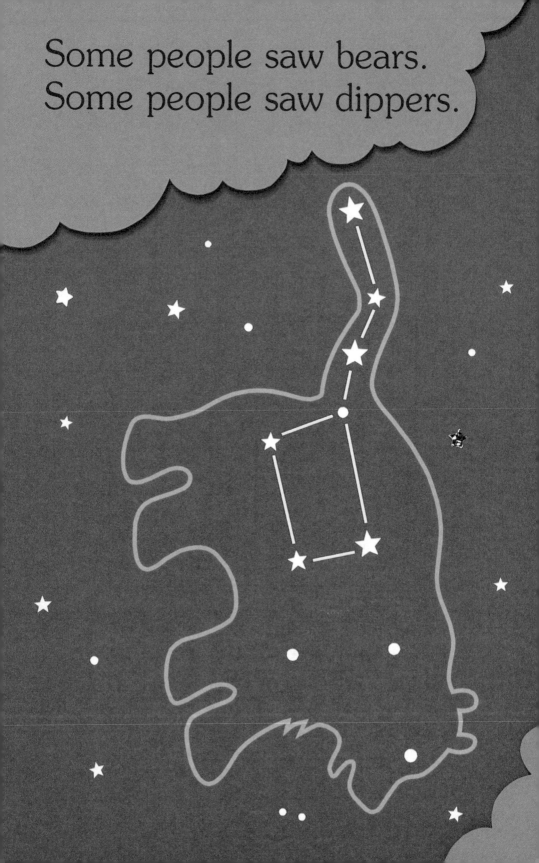

Some people saw bears.
Some people saw dippers.

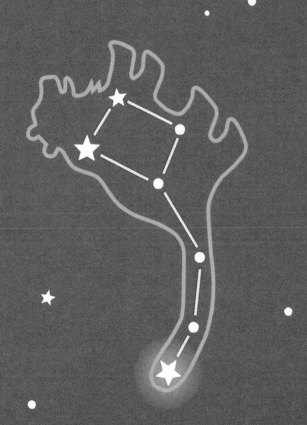

I am the last star
in the Little Dipper's handle.
Can you find me?
I am the North Star.
I am also called Polaris.

Wait a few months.
Look again.

All the stars have moved
except me!
Can you still see me?

I stay in the North.
Sailors use me
to find their way.

The sun is a star.
It is the star nearest to you.
It gives you heat and light.

The moon is not a star.
It reflects the light
of the sun.

To see stars better,
you need a telescope.

The study of stars
is called astronomy
[as-TRON-o-mee].
People who study stars
are called astronomers.
They use BIG telescopes.

How many ways
can you make a star?

USA

China

Israel

Puerto Rico

Some flags have stars.

Do you know a song
about a star?

When you wish upon a star,
what do you wish for?

# I Am an Apple

*For Martha and her apple tree*
*—J. Marzollo*

*For Dale, my friend and birthday mate*
*—J. Moffatt*

Text copyright © 1997 by Jean Marzollo.
Illustrations copyright © 1997 by Judith Moffatt.
All rights reserved. Published by Scholastic Inc.
SCHOLASTIC, HELLO READER, CARTWHEEL BOOKS and associated logos are trademarks and/or registered trademarks of Scholastic Inc.

Library of Congress Cataloging-in-Publication Data

Marzollo, Jean.
    I am an apple / by Jean Marzollo ; illustrated by Judith Moffatt.
        p.    cm.—(Hello reader! Level 1)
    "Cartwheel Books."
    Summary: Depicts a bud on an apple tree as it grows into an apple, ripens, is harvested, and provides seeds as a promise for the future.
    ISBN 0-590-37223-8
    1. Apples—Juvenile literature. 2. Apples—Life cycles—Juvenile literature. [1. Apples.]  I. Moffatt, Judith, ill.  II. Title.
III. Series.
SB363.M35     1997
634'.11—dc20                                                                97-6010
                                                                                  CIP
                                                                                   AC

# I Am an Apple

by Jean Marzollo
Illustrated by Judith Moffatt

## Hello Reader! Science — Level 1

SCHOLASTIC INC. Cartwheel BOOKS®

New York   Toronto   London   Auckland   Sydney
Mexico City   New Delhi   Hong Kong   Buenos Aires

I am a red bud.
I live on a branch
in an apple tree.

I grow in the rain.

I grow in the sun.

I unfold.

I'm an apple blossom!

I have five petals.
I am beautiful.

In time,

my petals

fall to the

ground.

Now I am a small apple.
I hang by a stem.
The stem brings me water
and food.

I grow
bigger

and
bigger.

My tree is full
of apples.

Once we were green.
Now we are red.
Red, redder, reddest.

Most apples
are picked
by farm workers.
Truckers drive
us to market.

Apples come in different shapes and colors.

Some are sweet.
Some are sour.

Applesauce is made
from apples.
What else is made
from apples?

Each apple has a
star of seeds inside.
The star has five parts,
just like the flower.

If you plant apple seeds,
what do you get?

Apple trees!

# I am an apple.

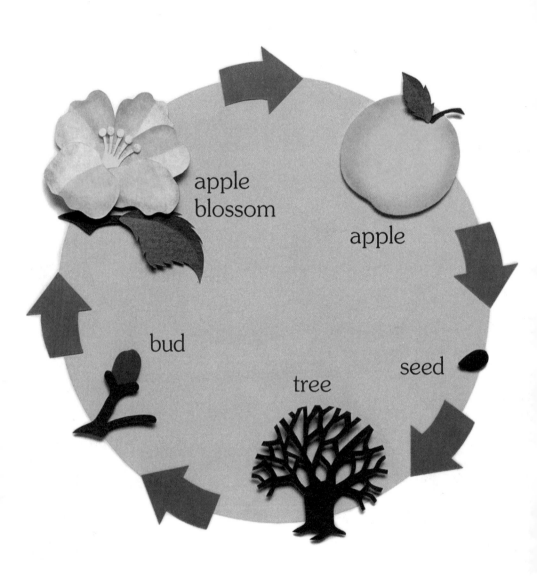

apple blossom

apple

bud

tree

seed

# Can you tell a story about me?

# I Am Snow

*For my Vermont Aunt Helen Martin McClausland*
*1909-1998*
*—J. Marzollo*

*To my confidantes: Kay, Ruth, Cheryl & Dale*
*—J. Moffatt*

Cut-paper photography by Paul Dyer.

**Go to www.scholastic.com for Web site information
on Scholastic authors and illustrators.**

Library of Congress Cataloging-in-Publication Data

Marzollo, Jean.
    I am snow / by Jean Marzollo; illustrated by Judith Moffatt.
        p.    cm. — (Hello reader! Science Level 1)
    Summary: Explains what snow is and what can be done with it.
Includes instructions for making a snowflake from paper.
    ISBN 0-590-64174-3
    1. Snow—Juvenile literature.    [1. Snow.]    I. Moffatt, Judith, ill.
    II. Title.    III. Series.
QC929.9.S7M37 1998
551.57'84—dc21                                                    98-17757
                                                                         CIP
                                                                         AC

# I Am Snow

by Jean Marzollo
Illustrated by Judith Moffatt

## Hello Reader ! Science — Level 1

SCHOLASTIC INC.
New York   Toronto   London   Auckland   Sydney
Mexico City   New Delhi   Hong Kong   Buenos Aires

I am not rain.
I do not drip,
            drip,
                  drip.

I am not hail.
I do not bounce,
   bounce,
      bounce.

I am not ice.
I do not crack,
 crack,
  crack.

I am snow.
I fall gently,
gently,
gently.

I am a million,
billion, trillion
snowflakes
all piled up.

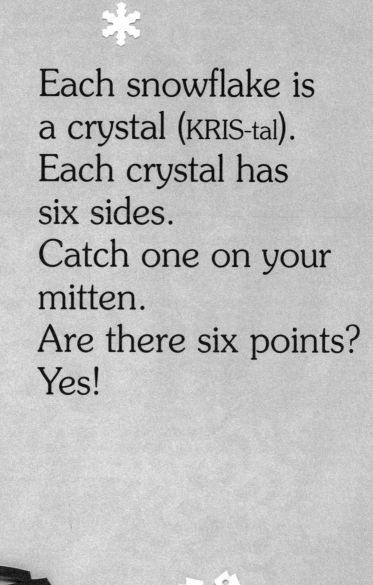

Each snowflake is
a crystal (KRIS-tal).
Each crystal has
six sides.
Catch one on your
mitten.
Are there six points?
Yes!

From afar,
all snowflakes look the same.
Up close,
you can see them better.
Each snowflake is different.

Some snow is wet
and sticky.
Wet snow makes good
snow people.

And snowballs!

Some snow is
dry and fluffy.
It is easy to shovel.

Who loves snow?
Skiers.
Snowboarders.

Snowshoe hikers.
Snow sliders.

Artists love snow, too.
This artist cut snowflakes
from tissue paper.
To find out how,
turn the page.

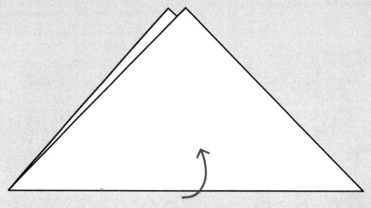

1. Fold a square of tissue paper in half
   to form a triangle.

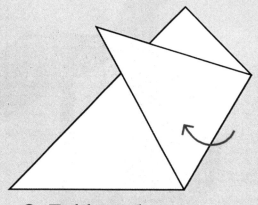

2. Fold up the
   right-hand corner.

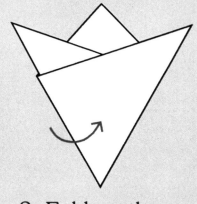

3. Fold up the
   left-hand corner.

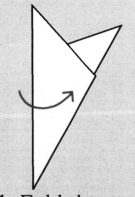

4. Fold this in half.

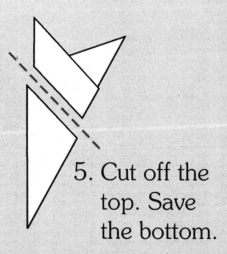

5. Cut off the
   top. Save
   the bottom.

6. Cut away pieces from
   all three sides.

7. Open!

What happens
to cold snow
in warm weather?
It melts.

Just like the rain,
it goes drip,
        drip,
            drip.

# I Am Water

*For Irene O'Garden and Walt Whitman*
*—J. Marzollo*

*For my niece Emma, with love*
*—J. Moffatt*

Text copyright © 1996 by Jean Marzollo.
Illustrations copyright © 1996 by Judith Moffatt.
All rights reserved. Published by Scholastic Inc.
SCHOLASTIC, HELLO READER, CARTWHEEL BOOKS and associated logos
are trademarks and/or registered trademarks of Scholastic Inc.

Library of Congress Cataloging-in-Publication Data

Marzollo, Jean.
    I am water / by Jean Marzollo ; illustrated by Judith Moffatt.
        p.    cm.—(Hello reader! Level 1)
    ISBN 0-590-26587-3
    1. Water—Juvenile literature. [1. Water.]    I. Moffatt, Judith, ill.
II. Title.  III. Series.
GB662.3. M37   1996
553.7—dc20                                                              95-10528
                                                                           CIP
                                                                           AC

# I Am Water

by Jean Marzollo
Illustrated by Judith Moffatt

## Hello Reader! Science—Level 1

SCHOLASTIC INC. Cartwheel B·O·O·K·S ®

New York   Toronto   London   Auckland   Sydney
Mexico City   New Delhi   Hong Kong   Buenos Aires

Watch me.
I am water.
I am home for the fish.

I am rain for the earth.

I am drink for the people.

I am bathwater for babies.

I am all that,
and I am more.

I am water for cooking.

I am ice for cooling.

I am snow for sledding.

I am pools for splashing.

I am all that,
and I am more.

I am puddles for boots.

I am rivers for boats.

I am lakes for swimming.

# I am waves for watching.

I am all that,
and I am more.

Watch me.
Watch over me.
I am water.